Rothenburg
OB ✳ DER ✳ TAUBER

Map &
Guide

D1089675

Dear Guests,

We would like you to get to know the magnificent sights of our city. Here are several suggestions from which you may choose:

Guided Tours: Daily from 1 April through 31 October and during the Christmas Market at 2.00 p.m. (in English)

Walking Tour with the Night Watchman: From 1 April through 30 December at 8.00 p.m. (in English)
starting at the Rathaus (Town Hall) main entrance on the Marktplatz (Market Square). Payments are to be made directly to the guide.

Discover the city on your own and take one of the following **walking tours**:
Tour 1 lasts approx. 2 hours
Tour 2 last approx. 4 hours and connects with Tour 1 at the Plönlein (Little Square).

Ⓐ **Rathaus (Town Hall):** The tour begins on the Marktplatz (Market Square), the center of urban life. The impressive Town Hall consists of two buildings. The Gothic part with its tower was erected between 1250 and 1400. The front part, a Renaissance building, was built between 1572 and 1578. Arcades were added in 1681. The coats of arms of the electoral princes decorate the front of the building. In the Middle Ages these electors elected the German King. Both buildings are connected by a courtyard. At the main entrance of the courtyard the old "Rothenburger Maße", the old measuring system, can be seen on both sides, left and right. During the Middle Ages even the smallest of states had its own measuring system which was publicly displayed on the Market Square. On the left you will see "Rute", "Elle" and "Schuh" and on the right the "Klafter". The Town Hall Tower is a remarkable piece of architecture since it has no foundations of its own, but only rests on top of the gable. In former times the tower accommodated the sentries who were to warn the city of fires and approaching enemies. The observation deck of the tower can be reached through the main entrance.

Ⓑ **Ratstrinkstube (City Councilors' Tavern):** This former tavern is probably one of the most famous buildings in Rothenburg and was only accessible to the City Councilors. A special attraction are the various clocks. The main clock was installed in 1683. Since 1910 the two windows to the right and left of the town clock open every hour between 11.00 a.m. and 3.00 p.m. and between 8.00 p.m. and 10.00 p.m. to show the legendary "Meistertrunk" (Master Draught). This legend goes back to the year 1631 when Catholic troops attacked and occupied Protestant Rothenburg. The Catholic General Tilly threatened to plunder and destroy the city. On a whim, he promised to spare the town from destruction, if a Councilor managed to empty an enormous tankard containing 3¼ liters of wine in one draught. The former mayor Nusch mastered this task and in doing so, he saved his city. Even today Rothenburg celebrates this rescue each year on Whitsun with a festival performance, grand army march and a field camp. Today this building accommodates the **Tourist Information.**
The picturesque St. George's Fountain (or Herterichs Well) is located on the south end of the Market Square. Due to the city's location on a plateau, its water supply was a major problem.

Over 40 fountains were built to ensure the water supply for both drinking and fire purposes. Cities in the Middle Ages were built with very narrow streets and the materials used made fires the greatest hazard for any community. The ① **St. George's Fountain** is 8 meters deep with a capacity of 100,000 liters and is the largest in the city. The fountain's decorations date back to the Late Renaissance (1608). Another attraction right next to the Town Hall is the Käthe Wohlfahrt Weihnachtsdorf, also called the "Christmas Village", which offers the largest selection of German Christmas decorations world wide and all year round in an enchanting atmosphere. Integrated into the "Christmas Village" you will find the

Ⓧ **German Christmas Museum**, a unique collection about the tradition of this family feast.

Walk through the courtyard of the Town Hall to reach the Ⓙ Historiengewölbe (Historical Vaults). This museum is dedicated to Rothenburg's difficult situation during the Thirty Years' War. Admire the old weapons and uniforms and, after descending the staircase through the vaults, you will find yourself in the former dungeons. Within these dungeon walls, Heinrich Toppler, the most powerful city mayor, died in 1408. After passing through the courtyard you will reach the "Grüner Markt", meaning Green Market, the former special market for vegetables. In front of you is now the largest church in the city of Rothenburg, the St. Jacob's Church.

Ⓒ **St. Jacob's Church**

The construction work of this Protestant church started in 1311. Almost two centuries passed before the church was consecrated in 1485. The largest church of this time reflects the city's wealth and the organized worship of God. St. Jacob's Church is famous for its altars, principally the "Heilig Blut Altar" (Holy Blood Altar) by Tilman Riemenschneider. The altar's name originates from a relic, a drop of Christ's blood. This relic turned Rothenburg into a major place of pilgrimage with a growing number of pilgrims in the Middle Ages. This altar was commissioned by the Town Council in 1500, in order to provide a worthy altar for this relic. It was to be created by the Würzburg altar carver Tilman Riemenschneider. The altar depicts the Last Supper, Christ's entry into Jerusalem and the scene at the Mount of Olives. It is one of the most magnificent altars in southern Germany. Another of Riemenschneider's works is the Louis de Toulouse Altar. Other remarkable works include the Altar of the Twelve Apostles by Friedrich Herlin and the large organ with 69 registers and 5,500 pipes.

A unique architectural feature of the church is that it was built over a lane. Go through the underpass of the church and find yourself in Klingengasse. A small lane on the left takes you to the Reichsstadtmuseum (Imperial City Museum).

Ⓞ **Reichsstadtmuseum (Imperial City Museum):** Rothenburg's local heritage museum is located inside the former Dominican Priory. From 1258 until the Reformation in 1544 nuns of this convent resided here. The size of the property speaks for the great economic importance of convents in the Middle Ages. The completely preserved priory kitchen dates back to this time. The collection of the museum also demonstrates the art and culture of the former Imperial City of Rothenburg with paintings depicting scenes from Christ's passion, the so-called "Rothenburg Passion", the museum gallery with paintings by artists of the 19th century and a remarkable "Judaika" (Jewish Heritage) department. The "Baumann Collection", consisting of faïences and weapons, receives special attention. Back in Klingengasse you turn left to find the "Klingentor" (Klingen Gate).

Ⓟ **Klingentor (Klingen Gate) and St. Wolfgangskirche (St. Wolfgang's Church):** The Klingen Tower was completed around 1400 and served as a water reservoir. Here is your first opportunity to climb the accessible part of the defense wall. Behind the Klingen Gate our attention is drawn to the Late Gothic style St. Wolfgang's Church, otherwise known as the Shepherds' Church. It was erected between 1475 and 1493 by a brotherhood of shepherds.

St. Wolfgang's Church is a fortress church with underground casemates and a rampart in the loft. The "Torwächterhaus" (Sentries' House) currently serves as the shepherds' dance chamber. Passing through the small arch on the left, you will reach the edge of the Tauber valley where it will be apparent to you just why the city was named "ob der Tauber". Rothenburg lies about 80 meters above the Tauber river. Here the fortifications aren't as extensive as in areas where flat land made enemy attacks easy. Look down into the valley and you will see a white tower, the so-called

Ⓩ **Topplerschlösschen (Toppler's Little Castle).** Built in 1388, it served as a resort for the powerful mayor Toppler. In this former moat castle he also met with King Wenzel.

(Should you be able to spend a little more time, we recommend a short hiking tour to the Tauber valley. An alley on the right leads down to the village of **Detwang**, the oldest part of the city of Rothenburg. As early as 960 a small village was built and in 968 the St. Peter-and-Paul's Church was erected. It is the only Romanesque style church in this region. During the 12th century, Gothic style elements were added. This church is known for its famous Holy Cross Altar by Tilman Riemenschneider.

The walkway along the outside of the defense wall takes you to the nucleus of the city, the so-called fortress.

Ⓜ **Burggarten (Castle Gardens):** Actually the name is a little misleading, since fortresses in the 12th century did not have gardens. It would be more correct to say "the gardens in the former place of the fortress". Here the Hohenstaufen family erected their Imperial Castle in 1142 and King Konrad III ruled his empire from this castle. King Konrad III was the only ruler to use the Rothenburg castle. Since both of his sons died very young, the castle lost its importance rather soon afterwards. However, the foundation for the city was laid. The community grew and spread over the hill until it became one of the ten largest cities of the Holy Roman Empire. Around the year 1400 it contained more than 6,000 inhabitants. In 1356 an earthquake destroyed the old castle. The remains of the castle's ruins provided valuable construction material that was used to build the city's defense wall. Only the **Blasiuskapelle (Chapel of St. Blaise)** was renovated after the earthquake. However, this building had not always been a chapel, but was first the "great house of the Dukes", probably serving as a conference building where the Emperor received his guests. Only after the renovation was it consecrated as a chapel. Today it serves as a memorial for the soldiers who died in the two world wars.

Enjoy a breathtaking view of the southern part of the city and the valley from the southern end of the gardens and see the so-called Kappenzipfel. In the valley you can admire the enormous Ⓨ **Doppelbrücke (Double Bridge)** which looks like an old Roman viaduct, despite its 14th century origin. Since Rothenburg is about 60 kilometers north of the Roman frontier fortifications, the Limes, Roman settlements and communities were unknown in the Rothenburg area.

Next to the bridge is the Ⓨ **Kobolzeller Kirche (Kobolzell Church)**, a Late Gothic style church which was erected between 1472 and 1501. During the Peasants' War in 1525, which was very severe in Rothenburg, the church's treasures were plundered. The Peasants' War lasted several months. One of the peasants' leaders, Florian Geyer, operated from Rothenburg. However, the princes defeated the peasants. Their 27 ringleaders were publicly executed on the Rothenburg Market Square.

When you turn to the Ⓛ **Burgtor (Castle Gate)**, you will see a mask on the gate from whose mouth hot pitch was poured onto attackers. A so-called needle-eye in the inner gate wing permitted only one person to pass at a time, so the large gate did not have to be opened during the hours of darkness. This would have been much too dangerous. In front of you is now Herrngasse, formerly the boulevard of Rothenburg, where the Patricians (the city's nobility) resided. Patricians governed the city for centuries. Today when you look at all the coats of arms on the houses, you will understand this lane's importance.

Ⓚ **Franziskanerkirche (Franciscan Church):** The former monastery church is the oldest church in Rothenburg. This Early Gothic style church was erected in 1285 and holds the Tilman Riemenschneider St. Francis Altar. Back on the Market Square turn right just past St. George's Fountain into Hofbronnengasse. To your right you will find the

1544	The Reformation occurs in Rothenburg.

1544   The Reformation occurs in Rothenburg.

1618–1648   During the Thirty Years' War, Protestant Rothenburg is occupied several times.
In 1631 the so-called "Meistertrunk" (Master Draught) saves the city from destruction.

1802   After 500 years of independence, the Franconian Rothenburg is reluctantly annexed to the Bavarian Kingdom.

1945   The city is victim of a bombing attack by the allied forces. The eastern part of the city is destroyed and a total of over 40% of the old buildings goes up in flames.

Generous financial support from all over the world enabled the destroyed areas to be restored. It is still protected by exemplary preservation laws.

Museums and Sights (Daily Opening Hours)

Ⓐ **Town Hall/Town Hall Tower:** Apr.–Oct. 9.30 a.m.–12.30 p.m., 1.00 p.m.–5.00 p.m., Nov., Jan.–Mar. Sat./Sun., 12.00 a.m.–3.00 p.m., Dec. 12.00 a.m.– 3.00 p.m.

Ⓒ **St. Jacob's Church:** Apr.–Oct. 9.00 a.m.–5.15 p.m., Dec. 10.00 a.m.–5.00 p.m., Nov., Jan.–Mar. 10.00 a.m.–12.00 a.m., 2.00 p.m.–4.00 p.m.

Ⓕ **Craftsmen's House:** Easter-Weekend–Oct. 31: Mon.–Fri. 11.00 a.m.–5.00 p.m., Sat./Sun. 10.00 a.m.–5.00 p.m., Nov. 1–Jan. 7: 2.00 p.m.–4.00 p.m., Jan. 8–Easter-Weekend closed.

Ⓗ **Doll and Toy Museum:** Mar.–Dec. 9.30 a.m.–6.00 p.m., Jan, Feb. 11.00 a.m.–5.00 p.m.

Ⓙ **Historical Vaults:** April–Oct. 9.30 a.m.–5.30 p.m., Jan.–Mar. + Nov. closed, Christmas Market 1.00 p.m.–4.00 a.m.

Ⓚ **Franciscan Church:** Feb.–Dec. 10.00 a.m.–12.00 a.m., 2.00 p.m.–4.00 p.m.

Ⓝ **Medieval Crime Museum:** Apr.–Oct. 9.30 a.m.–6.00 p.m., Nov., Jan., Feb. 2.00 p.m.–4.00 p.m., Dec. + March10.00 a.m.–4.00 p.m.

Ⓞ **Imperial City Museum:** Apr. – Oct. 10.00 a.m.–5.00 p.m., Nov. – Mar. 1.00 p.m.–4.00 p.m.

Ⓟ **St. Wolfgang's Church:** Apr.–Oct. 10.00 a.m.–5.00 p.m., also on weekends during the Christmas Market.

Ⓧ **German Christmas Museum:** Mid April–Mid Jan. 10.00 a.m.–5.30 p.m., Mid Jan.–Mid April only Sat. + Sun. 10.00 a.m.–5.30 p.m., closed on Good Friday, opened on Christmas and Boxing Day as well as on Jan. 1.

Ⓩ **Toppler's Little Castle:** Nov. closed, year round Fri. – Sun. 1.00 p.m.–4.00 p.m.

St. Peter and Pauls's Church, Detwang: Apr., May, Sep. 8.30 a.m.–12.00 a.m., 1.30 a.m.–5.00 p.m., Jun – Aug. 8.30 a.m.–12.00 a.m., 1.30 p.m.–6.00 p.m., Nov. – Mar. (except Mondays) 10.00 a.m.–12.00 a.m., 2.00 p.m.–4.00 p.m.

Subject to change

Further information:

Rothenburg Tourist Office
Marktplatz 2
91541 Rothenburg ob der Tauber
Tel. +49-9861-404-800
Fax +49-9861-404-529
www.rothenburg.de
E-Mail: info@rothenburg.de

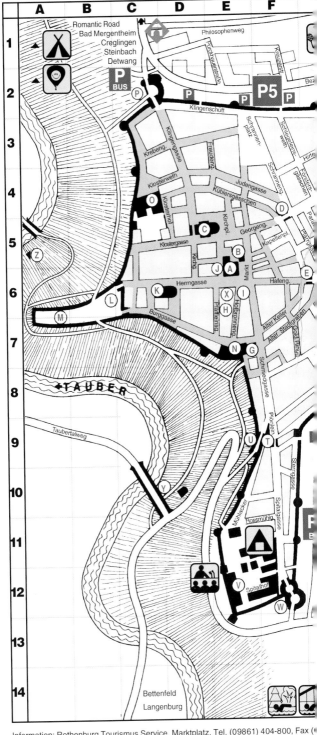

Information: Rothenburg Tourismus Service, Marktplatz, Tel. (09861) 404-800, Fax (
Printed: Schneider Druck GmbH, 91541 Rothenburg o. d. T., Tel. (09861) 400-0
Mai 2005, Cover photo: Willi Sauer

plaques with names and meter inscriptions. These identify the donors who financed the renovation of the defense wall after this part was destroyed during the aerial bombing on 31 March 1945. The eastern part of the city was also totally destroyed. The reconstruction of this part took almost 20 years. Thanks to God, the center and the western part of the city remained almost undamaged.

About 300 meters further down, right next to the wall you can admire the Ⓢ **Gerlachschmiede (Old Forge)**, a building with an extremely charming ornamental half-timbered gable. Until 40 years ago, the forge was still in use.

The next large gate you will pass is the Ⓡ **Rödertor (Röder Gate)**. Built towards the end of the 14th century it is flanked by the customs building and a guards' house. This is where we leave the wall to walk back to Market Square via Rödergasse. On your way there, discover one of the most beautiful "gate motifs", the Ⓔ **Markusturm (Markus Tower) and Röderbogen (Röder Arch)**. Both were built around 1200 when the first city wall (inner circle) was erected. Behind the Markus Tower and Röder Arch is the former "Büttelhaus", one of the former city prisons. Today the Büttelhaus is the city's archive. Right before the Röder Arch there is an alley on your left that leads you down to the old city moat. This is where the Ⓕ **Alt-Rothenburger-Handwerkerhaus (Old Rothenburg Craftsmen's House)** is located. It was built in 1270 and gives you insight into how a craftsman and his large family lived and worked in the Middle Ages. The house contains eleven originally furnished rooms.

You will reach Galgengasse (Gallows Lane) through Pfarrgasse. This lane was named Galgengasse because in former times it led to the place of execution. The imposing gate at the right end of the lane is therefore named Galgentor (Gallows Gate). To your left is Ⓓ **Weißer Turm (White Tower)** a 12th century city gate. Right next to the White Tower is the former Judentanzhaus (Jews' Dance Hall), the center of Jewish life in the Middle Ages. Rothenburg, like many other free imperial cities, had a large Jewish community. At times Jews composed 20 % of the city's total population. The Talmud School of the famous Rabbi Meir Ben Baruch had a world wide reputation. Jewish tomb stones from the Middle Ages are integrated into the garden's wall.

You will find your way back to the Market Square by walking through Georgengasse. We hope that this walking tour gave you a good first impression of Rothenburg.

Brief History of the City

960	First community in Detwang in the Tauber valley.
1142	Erection of the Imperial Castle (lat. "Castrum Imperiale") by the Hohenstaufen King Konrad III. A community, later named Rothenburg, develops on the hill next to the castle.
1167	After the death of Friedrich, Duke of Rothenburg, the castle is abandoned. Thanks to its geographic location, the city develops over the years into a commercial center.
1274	King Rudolf of Habsburg elevates Rothenburg to a Free Imperial City.
1356	An earthquake destroys the entire imperial castle and parts of the city.
1400	The city experiences its heyday under mayor Toppler. With over 6000 inhabitants, Rothenburg is one of the largest cities of the empire.
1525	The city allies itself to the rebels' leader, Florian Geyer, during the Peasants' War. The city's decline begins.

(H) **Puppen- und Spielzeugmuseum (The Doll and Toy Museum)** where over 300 dolls from the time between 1780 and 1940 are displayed in an area of 400 square meters. Doll's houses, doll's rooms, doll's kitchens, shops and metal toys take you back to bygone childhood days. About 100 meters further down is the probably most important museum of Rothenburg.

(N) **Mittelalterliches Kriminalmuseum (The Medieval Crime Museum):** It is located inside the building of the former Commander of the Order of St. John built in 1395, and was altered in 1718 to a Baroque style building. The famous law and law enforcement museum gives you insight to 1000 years of European legal history in an easy to understand way. Covering four floors and an area of 2000 square meters you will learn about the nature of law enforcement of this era and the punishments that people had to expect for even minor offenses. Right next to the museum on the left is the

(G) **Johanniskirche (St. John's Church)** which is one of the town's Catholic churches and was erected between 1390 and 1410. Formerly, one of the gates of the first city wall was incorporated in the eastern gable. Having left the museum you are now in Schmiedgasse where you can view one of the most famous sights in Rothenburg.

(T) **Plönlein (Little Square):** The Plönlein is one of the most charming medieval sights in Germany. Two important access ways form a small triangular square with one small road coming from the right, directly from the Tauber valley Double Bridge. Another comes from the left, the southern part of suburban Rothenburg. Siebersturm (Siebers Tower), which is just behind Plönlein, dates back to around 1385 and was part of the second fortification, an extension of the first. The smaller gate towards the valley on the right is called

(U) **Kobolzeller Tor (Kobolzell Gate)** and was built around 1360. It is part of one of the most interesting fortifications in Rothenburg with its own inner courtyard and formerly four gates.

This is where walking tour 1 ends. Find your way back to the Market Square through Schmiedgasse.

Walking tour 2 takes you on to the southern part of the city.
Enter the so-called "Kappenzipfel", the southern part of the city through Siebers Tower and you will reach Spitalgasse. The name "Spitalgasse" (Hospital Lane) originates from the former hospital which is located at the end of this lane. A right turn takes you to **Rossmühle (Nag's Mill)**, a very solid building from 1516. Nag's Mill was a horse-driven mill that took 16 horses to operate in case the city was under siege. Today it is one of Germany's most beautiful youth hostels. The "Spital", the former hospital was originally located outside the city wall and was not integrated into the town until the 15th century. Inside the Spital courtyard is the "Hegereiterhaus", the former residence of the hospital administrator. It was built during the 16th century. On the lower end of the Spital courtyard is the former "Zehntscheune", a barn dating from 1699, where peasants had to pay their taxes in kind. In 1975 the barn was converted into the (V) **Reichsstadthalle (Imperial City Festival Hall)** offering a historic setting for international congresses and other events.

(W) **Spitalbastei (Spital Bastion)** The southern end of the city wall is the most imposing bulwark of Rothenburg. The bastion was built during the 17th century and has two inner courtyards, seven gates and an upper walkway with embrasures. The well preserved and imposing dry moat shows that not only walls protected the city. Oftentimes attackers failed during the attempt to cross the moats.

Walk a short way back on Spitalgasse. After about 100 meters you will discover a gap in the wall where you can climb the stairs to the defense wall. As you stroll along the sentry walk you will find several small

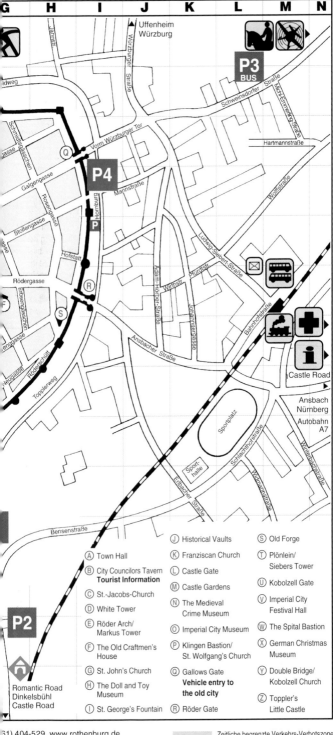

A Town Hall

B City Councilors Tavern
   Tourist Information

C St.-Jacobs-Church

D White Tower

E Röder Arch/
   Markus Tower

F The Old Craftmen's
   House

G St. John's Church

H The Doll and Toy
   Museum

I St. George's Fountain

J Historical Vaults

K Franziscan Church

L Castle Gate

M Castle Gardens

N The Medieval
   Crime Museum

O Imperial City Museum

P Klingen Bastion/
   St. Wolfgang's Church

Q Gallows Gate
   **Vehicle entry to
   the old city**

R Röder Gate

S Old Forge

T Plönlein/
   Siebers Tower

U Kobolzell Gate

V Imperial City
   Festival Hall

W The Spital Bastion

X German Christmas
   Museum

Y Double Bridge/
   Kobolzell Church

Z Toppler's
   Little Castle

61) 404-529, www.rothenburg.de   Zeitliche begrenzte Verkehrs-Verbotszone

Rothenburg

Evening sky above Rothenburg ob der Tauber

Guide to the
town´s most beautiful sights

VERLAG &
MEDIADESIGN

Heidelberg / Dielheim

Contents

Notes

_____

_____

_____

_____

_____

_____

_____

_____

_____

_____

_____

_____

_____

_____

_____

_____

_____

Your tips and suggestions are always welcome, as they help us keep this guide up to date.

Welcome to Rothenburg!

Rothenburg, the former free imperial town, is one of the most well-known German towns internationally and certainly one of the most visited. It is located at the intersection of Burgenstrasse and the Romantic Road on a plain 425 metres above sea level. The Tauber river flows in its valley cut 60 metres deep at the foot of the town, hence the "ob (oberhalb, above) der (the) Tauber" in the name of Rothenburg. Its 12,500 inhabitants living within and outside the town walls are employed mainly in the tourist sector. Rothenburg has 24 hotels, 35 inns and guest-houses and numerous private landlords offering a total of over 2,000 beds. There are 90 restaurants, wine taverns and cafés catering for guests in the town.

Rothenburg ob der Tauber – medieval gem

Apart from taking in the countless sights of our beautiful medieval town, you should also go on excursions, walks and hikes in its attractive surroundings. You can take part in guided theme hikes or follow the well-signposted footpaths, or cycle along the signposted cycle paths in the valley of the Tauber or over the Frankenhöhe to Altmühl. Sports enthusiasts can enjoy tennis, riding, fishing, bowling, shooting, flying a private plane or swimming in the heated forest swimming pool with its ozone roofed-over baths. There are also three golf courses nearby. From April to September, you can watch genuine American Football of federal league class on the league playing days. Rothenburg offers a wealth of cultural attractions at many weekends, particularly during the warmer part of the year. The events and festivals include the Taubertal Openair.

History of Rothenburg ob der Tauber

10th c.   Castle Grafenburg built

1108   The line of the counts dies out. Heinrich von Rothenburg bequeaths his seat to Comburg Monastery.

1116   Emperor HeinrichV invests his nephew Herzog Konrad von Schwaben with the castle settlement. Rothenburg thereby passes into the possession of the Hohenstaufen Emperors.

1137   Konrad crowned king

1142   Building of castle Hohenstaufenburg Rothenburg ("castrum imperiale")

1152   Konrad dies. His nephew Friedrich I "Barbarossa" becomes king, as Konrad's son Friedrich, "the Child of Rothenburg", is only eight years old.

1157   The 13-year-old Friedrich von Rothenburg is knighted and designated Duke von Rothenburg.

1167   Friedrich "the Handsome" von Rothenburg helps his cousin Friedrich I expel Pope Alexander III from Rome. He dies there during an epidemic. Rothenburg passes to Emperor Friedrich, who has it administered by bailiffs.

12th c.   Building of the first town wall. The Burgtor, Weisser Turm, Markusturm and Röderbogen are still preserved today.

1258   Founding of a Dominican convent (for aristocrats)

1274   Rothenburg becomes a free imperial town under King Rudolf von Habsburg.

First extension of the town wall to include the newly created residential quarters of the craftsmen within the protection of the fortifications.

1339	Rothenburg is authorized by Emperor Ludwig the Bavarian to form alliances independently.
1356	The entire castle complex is destroyed, probably in an earthquake. There is no written source on this event. Only the "High House of the Dukes", the Blasiuskapelle, remains preserved up to the present day.
From 1311	Construction of the church St.-Jakobs-Kirche, consecrated in 1485
14th c.	With the second town extension, the hospital quarter is included as "Kappenzipfel" ("Tip of the Cap") in the ring of fortifications.
Ca. 1400	Heyday of Rothenburg under the great Mayor Toppler, commander of the towns Ulm, Nördlingen and Dinkelsbühl
1407	War between towns; Rothenburg is besieged by the burgrave Friedrich von Nürnberg and the Bishop of Würzburg. Property outside the town walls is devastated.
1408	Peace of Mergentheim, imposing very harsh terms on the people of Rothenburg. Mayor Toppler is taken prisoner and dies in the dungeon.
1451	Revolt of craftsmen against the council of the patricians
1501	The eastern part of the town hall is destroyed by a fire.
1525	Peasants' War: Rothenburg allies with the peasant leader Florian Geyer. Its defeat by a princes' army is followed by the holding of a criminal court by the margrave Casimir von Ansbach and a mass execution.

Tilly, commander of the imperial forces in the Thirty Years' War. His conquest of Rothenburg in 1631 is associated with the legend of the "Master Draught" ("Meistertrunk").

1544   Rothenburg finally introduces the Protestant service.

1572   Laying of the foundation stone for the town hall in Renaissance style, Rothenburg's most important building

1618–48   Thirty Years' War. The Protestant –"Union" convenes in Rothenburg in 1618. The town is besieged and taken by Tilly in 1631, by Piccolomini in 1634 and by Turenne in 1645. According to legend, the "Master Draught" performed by Nusch saves Rothenburg from destruction in 1631. The free imperial town of Rothenburg becomes politically insignificant due to the burdens of war.

1688   A French tax-raising army under General Fenquiéres destroys mills and villages around Rothenburg.

1802   Rothenburg annexed by Bavaria

1873   The town gains the rail connection it needed.

In 19th c.   Rothenburg is "discovered" by artists such as Richter and Spitzweg.

1945	Rothenburg is partially destroyed (approx. 40%) in an air raid, although its historic centre remains unscathed. The complete destruction of the town is prevented by John McCloy, later the first US High Commissioner for Germany.
After 1945	Reconstruction of Rothenburg in its original style. The destroyed fortifications are rebuilt with the support of friends of the town and sponsors from all over the world.
1975	Extension of the "Zehntscheune" (warehouse for a tenth of the harvest) of the hospital into the Reichsstadthalle (imperial town hall)
1982	Opening of the Imperial Town Museum in the former Dominican convent. This exhibits numerous art treasures, the showpiece being Baumann's weapons' collection, one of the most important weapons' collections in south Germany from the Middle Ages to the modern age, the convent kitchen and the Indaica (Jewish department).
1985	700th anniversary of the Franciscan church, Rothenburg's oldest church
1985	Connection to motorway A7, stimulating the town's economy and tourist trade
1993	700th anniversary of the death of Rabbi Meir ben Baruch von Rothenburg
1998	Old Rothenburg Association celebrates its 100th anniversary
1998	Inauguration of memorial stone commemorating the Jewish persecution of 1298 in the Burggarten
2004	500th anniversary of the completion of the Holy Blood Altar by Tilman Riemenschneider

1 Market square/town councillorrs´ tavern

Even in early times, the market square, flanked by venerable patrician houses, was the venue of key events in Rothenburg's history. From his throne in front of the town councillors' tavern (with the town clock), Emperor Friedrich III invested King Christian of Denmark with Holstein in 1474. And here on June 30th 1525 the margrave Casimir von Ansbach had 21 agitators from the Peasants' War publicly beheaded. According to the chronicle, "the blood ran like a stream down Schmiedgasse."

On October 31st 1631, the women and children of Rothenburg fell down on their knees in front of Tilly, who

had been enraged by the town's resistance, and begged for mercy. The army of Gustav Adolph camped here in 1632.

Today, the market square is still the lively centre of the town and the starting-place for tours. The historic Shepherds' Dance and the Entry of the Imperial Troops are enacted here (see the section on events). On the Imperial Town Festival days, the market square provides a fitting backdrop for the fireworks display accompanied by music celebrating the entry of the citizens.

The town hall steps are a welcome place for sitting down not only for these festivities: they are really inviting for visitors keen to rest their weary feet after pounding the pavements – and enjoy watching the constant hustle and bustle here in the centre of Rothenburg, at the intersection of the old lanes.

View from the town hall terrace over the market square

Town councillors´tavern

Look up at the steep baroque gable crowned by the belfry and you'll notice above the main town clock (1683) a calendar clock and then the imperial eagle and a sundial. Figures representing the main protagonists in the "Master Draught" legend from the time of the Thirty Years' War appear in the two windows to the right and left of the town clock at the following times: 11 am, 12 am, 1 pm, 2 pm and 3 pm, as well as 8 pm, 9 pm and 10 pm. According to the "Master Draught" legend, Tilly was able to take Rothenburg only after fierce resistance on October 30th 1631. The town was to be plundered and destroyed and the councillors executed. The next day, the cellarman offered Tilly a tankard with 3 1/4 litres of the heavy Franconian wine as a welcoming drink. The commander announced that he would spare the town if one of the councillors emptied the tankard at a single draught. The former mayor Nusch performed this feat in ten minutes and thus saved Rothenburg. Although he slept afterwards for three days on end, Nusch lived for another 37 years, dying at the age of 80.

Gable of the town councillors' tavern with the main town clock flanked by Nusch performing the "Master Draught" (r.) and General Tilly

2 Town hall

The market square is dominated by the impressive Renaissance facade of the town hall with the baroque arcades in front. The old Gothic part of the twin building with the gable tower, over 50 metres high, is behind. The construction of the present building began in 1250, after the old Gothic town hall had burnt down ten years previously. The Gothic twin building as portrayed on a contemporary painting on the back of the Altar of the Twelve Apostles in the Jakobskirche was completed at the end of the 14th c. The front part was destroyed by fire in 1501. The splendid Renaissance section was added in its place between 1572 and 1578. A major part in this project was played by the Rothenburg stonemason and sculptor Leonhard Weidmannder.

Town hall with Renaissance building (16th c.) with arcades in front

Town hall

Opening hours:
Daily 8 am-6 pm, no admission charged
Town hall tower: April-Oct. daily
9.30 am-12.30 am and 1 pm-5 pm. Nov, Jan.-March
Sat., Sun. 12 am-3 pm, Dec. daily 12 am-3 pm

View of market square from town hall

The arcades were not added in front of the town hall until 1681. The architects of the time were expert at harmoniously combining the components of three different stylistic eras with one another. The severe horizontal line of the German Renaissance is interrupted by the stairway tower and the high corner oriel and thus adapted to the Gothic building, striving upwards to the heavens.

Above: Stairway portal to Renaissance town hall

Left: Renaissance portal in inner courtyard

Below: Courtyard between town hall buildings

Inside the town hall

The artistic spiral staircase in the stairway tower takes us up into the spacious lobby of the first upper floor, which is spanned by a heavy wooden-beamed ceiling. The coats of arms of the Rothenburg patrician families, such as von Staudt, Nusch, Bezold and Winterbach, are on the right and left of the Renaissance portal of the stairway tower. One of the paintings depicts the most famous mayor of Rothenburg and commander of the imperial towns, Heinrich Toppler, in knight's armour. There is a bronze plaque portraying Gustav Adolph, who stayed the night here a few weeks before his death in October 1632. Via the central portal opposite the stairway tower, we come into the Gothic "Kaisersaal" (imperial room), which is well worth seeing. The giant wooden-beamed ceiling of this room features a ceiling joist. The Renaissance benches in front of the windows, the railings on the stairs and the relief presentation of the Last Judgement are all artistically carved of stone. These also include the court bars, which are installed today in the vestibule in front of the hall. The vault of the stairway tower is adorned with magnificent Gothic tracery. Around the imperial eagle are grouped the coats of arms of the electors and the town, as well as the monogram of the architect Weidmann. Via the top storey, we come to the town hall tower. Its lookout gallery provides a splendid view over Rothenburg's sea of houses, countless towers and fortifications. There is a picturesque Renaissance portal, possibly a work by Weidmann, in the southern part of the courtyard between the buildings. This was the main entrance until the new part of the town hall was completed in 1578.

Below: Bars
Right: Town hall, Kaisersaal with relief of the Last Judgement

3 Herterichsbrunnen

The south-west corner of the market square features Rothenburg's most beautiful fountain, Herterichs- or St.-Georgs-Brunnen. As early as 1446, water of a spring was fed via a canal system into the town to supply the inhabitants. The richly decorated dodecagonal fountain was given its present form by the Rothenburg sculptor Christoph Körner, who designed it in Renaissance style in 1608. The centre pillar with the shields is crowned by the figure of St. George. The symbols of medieval justice, including gallows and pillory, used to be set up in front of the fountain. The shepherds of the surrounding countryside danced around this once a year to protect Rothenburg from the plague. According to another legend, they danced for joy about a treasure that a shepherd had discovered in a dream.

The half-timbered house alongside, called Jagstheimerhaus, today the chemist's Marien-Apotheke, was built in 1488 for Mayor Jagstheimer. There is a figure of the Holy Virgin under the romantic oriel. The picturesque dreamy inner court with the richly adorned breasts of the galleries is exemplary for the patrician courts of that time. The Jagstheimerhaus once accommodated emperors, including Maximilian I in 1513. With the Baumeisterhaus, it is one of the most beautiful patrician houses in Rothenburg. The garret also became famous by being featured in the painting of the impoverished poet by the well-known artist Spitzweg.

Herterichsbrunnen: Renaissance fountain with figure of St. George, hence called St.-Georgs-Brunnen. L.: Jagstheimerhaus, Marien-Apotheke, r.: town hall

Baumeisterhaus (1956), Renaissance building built by Weidmann, adjoining on the right the house of the mayor (Toppler, 14th c.)

On the south-east corner, Obere Schmiedgasse leads into the market square. The first three patrician houses we see feature the architectural styles of various eras.

The Gasthof zum Greifen was the domicile of Mayor Toppler.

The picturesque inner court in the Baumeisterhaus served the patricians as extended living area during the warm part of the year.

The building was built towards the end of the 14th c., although the gable was renewed in the 17th c. Towards the market square, it is adjoined by the most magnificent middle-class house in Rothenburg, the Baumeisterhaus, designed by Leonhard Weidmann in Renaissance style in 1596 for the municipal architect of the day. The steps of the gable are harmoniously adorned by scrolls in the form of dragons.

The window supports of the two upper floors with alternating figures of men and women representing the seven virtues and the seven vices are particularly striking. In the bottom row, for instance, we see kind-heartedness, gluttony, motherliness and fraud represented next to one another. Another interesting sight is the picturesque inner courtyard, which is preserved in its original state and is now used as a café.

The neighbouring house decorated with coats of arms with the stepped gable used to be a chemist's.

Schmiedgasse is enlivened by artistically designed signs of shops and guest houses as well as floral decoration on the house fronts.

5 Art exhibition in the Meat and Dancing House

The high-gabled half-timbered building behind the fountain, the Meat and Dancing House, rests on the foundation walls of the old town hall, which burnt down in 1240. The Rothenburg butchers sold their wares in the basement up into the 18th c. Today, the Meat and Dancing House accommodates the exhibition of paintings by the numerous artists represented in Rothenburg. Most of the works can be purchased.

Imperial Town Meat and Dancing House with Herterichsbrunnen, r. Jagstheimerhaus and town hall oriel

Festivities used to be held in the large hall above the cross vaults. This building served as cloth hall, in which the uniforms of the militias used to be kept, and it is still used today as clothing depot for festivities. The historic Shepherds' Dance is not performed around the fountain as in the past, but in front of the town hall several times a year (see events).

Meat and Dancing House on market square

Opening hours:
April-Oct. daily 10 am-5 pm,
also during "Winter fairy tale"
Admission free

---

6 Histirical Vaults and dungeons

Diagonally opposite the Meat and Dancing House is the entrance to the courtyard and the Historical Vaults presenting an exhibition of items and scenes from the time of the Thirty Years' War, as well as utensils of the historic festival performance of the "Master Draught". The vaults used to accommodate grocery shops, in which mainly dealers from outside offered their wares and which sold the few goods not reserved for the craftsmen. Accompanied by the caretaker, we come to the dungeons, two floors under the Kaisersaal. Next to the old torture chamber are three dark, cramped dungeons, where Heinrich Toppler, his oldest son Jakob and his cousin languished in 1408. While Toppler himself died (possibly executed) two months later on June 13th, his relatives were released the following month after appeals made by friends. Toppler's heirs had to sell their property in Rothenburg and leave the town for ever. After paying a fine of over 10,000 gulden, they moved to Nuremberg.

We leave the courtyard at the other end and approach the

main church St. Jakob, before which we first turn right.

Historical Vaults: Mercenaries playing dice, scene from the Thirty Years' War

Historical Vaults
Entrance town hall, courtyard

Opening hours:
April-Oct. 9.30 am-5.30 pm,
during Christmas Market 1 pm-4 pm
Jan., March, Nov. closed

7 Old Grammar School

The imposing Renaissance building with the octagonal stairway tower on the north side of Kirchplatz is the former Latin School (1589). The giant attic served as a grain store. The large wine cellar under the Old Grammar School is just as impressive.

Today the building is used by the church as a community centre.

Old Grammar School (1589) with stairway tower

View from Bettenfeld in the south-west

8 Jakobskirche

Let's now turn to Rothenburg's main church, the Jakobskirche, built in High Gothic style over a period of more than a hundred years and consecrated in 1448. The colossal structure with its towers with perforated spires dominates the town. Viewed close up, it offers an impressive example of Gothic ecclesiastical architecture with narrow windows, flying buttresses and towers directing the view upwards, to God.

St.-Jakobs-Kirche: Main church of Rothenburg built in High Gothic style (14th/15th c.) with different spires

Romantic view of St.-Jakobs-Kirche, r. the "Reichsküchenmeister" (imperial head cook), former seat of the Hohenstaufen imperial administrators

St.-Jakobs-Kirche

Opening hours:
April-Oct. daily 9 am-5.30 pm,
Dec. 10 am-5 pm, Nov.,
Jan.-March 10 am-12 am and 2 pm-4 pm

The Teutonic Order had the Jakobskirche built on the site of the old parish church, which was still a branch church of the older settlement Detwang. The project was, however, financed by the citizens of Rothenburg. Owing to the long construction time, many master craftsmen were involved in the planning and building work.

Legend has it that the southern tower was built by the master himself and the leaner northern tower by his journeyman. The master was said to

Southern tower of the Jakobskirche

have been so infuriated by the superior workmanship of his journeyman that he threw himself off his tower, plunging down to his death.

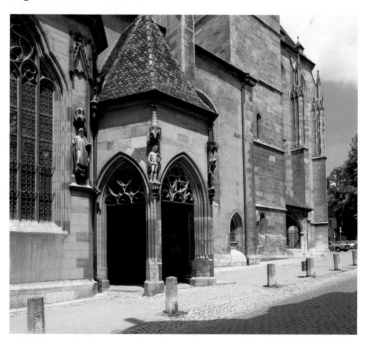

Richly decorated "Brautportal" on the southern side of the church

We enter the Jakobskirche through the southern portal – somewhat to the right of which is the richly decorated "Brauttür". This is already impressive from the outside, but the interior is all the more imposing with its wealth of exemplary elements of the high art of German Gothic, which devoted its tremendous creative energy almost exclusively to sacred architecture.

Pointed arcades link the centre aisle, 24 metres high, with the low side aisles. Above the arcades, light wall areas are predominant, interrupted only by the lean upwardly striving pillars, which without capitals lead over to the simple cross vault.

St.-Jakobs-Kirche: Nave and choir with Altar of the Twelve Apostles and colourful medieval windows

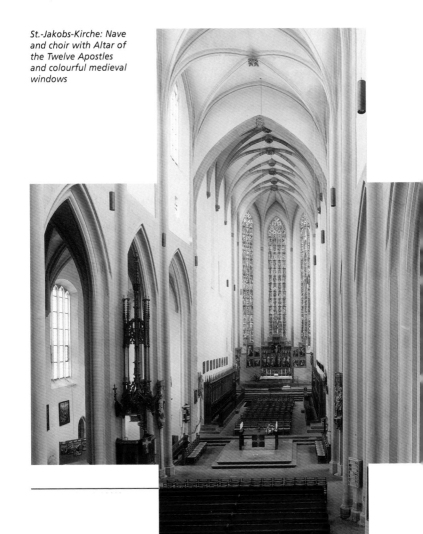

Works of art in the church interior

Under the gallery, we find in the southern side aisle a presentation of the prophet Elijah. Towards the choir on the outer wall are the rear sides of a former winged altarpiece, a gravestone and, at the opening to the chapel Spörleinkapelle, a Late Gothic figure of the Holy Virgin. The following chapel is dedicated to the great mayor Heinrich Toppler (d. 1408), who left this church important gifts.

Passing a figure of St. James and the Hornburg Epitaph, we come at the end of the side aisle to the Coronation of Mary Altar, completed around 1520 by an unknown master, probably from the Riemenschneider school. The coronation of Mary is presented in the shrine and underneath – in the predella – Mary's death, which presents an old farm-house room portrayed in the most minute detail. Anna Selbdritt (Anna, Mary and Jesus, a frequent presentation in the Late Middle Ages) and Mary with child are presented on the wings. The filigree Gothic backdrop was stored separately for many years and has adorned the altar again for some time.

The first column is decorated by four notable stone sculptures of St. Christopher, George, John the Baptist and John the Evangelist.

We enter the raised choir area, created between 1311 and 1322 and thus the oldest part of the church. A figure of Peter welcomes us at the level of the steps. The choir stalls were crafted by a Rothenburg master in 1514 for the members of the Teutonic Order. Over them hang portraits of former main preachers of the Jakobskirche after the Reformation.

The choir area is dominated by the main altar of the church, the magnificent Altar of the Twelve Apostles, one of the most important high altars in Germany. It was completed in 1466, financed by a generous donation. The superb sculptures in the shrine are the work of Swabian masters.

Above: Altar of the Twelve Apostles with the Apostles in the predella
Below: Presentation of the Jesus child in the Temple

The most impressive feature is the crucifix, surrounded by four angels. Next to this we can identify to the left Mary, James (the church's patron saint) and Elisabeth, and on the right John, Leonhard and Anthony. The lower part shows Jesus among his disciples, giving the altar its name. The paintings are all from the workshop of Friedrich Herlin, who worked mainly in Nördlingen. The inner sides of the wings feature pictures from the life of Mary:

Birth of Jesus, visit of the Three Magi

Death of Mary

Jesus in the Temple

1. Annunciation and Visitation, Birth of Christ and Circumcision, r. Adoration by the Magi, Christ in the Temple and – on two panels – Mary's Death. The outer sides show the death and legend of St. James. When the altar wings are closed, the presentation is as follows:

1. Sermon and arrest, 2. Execution and 3. Transfer of the body into a medieval town. Then follow scenes from the legend of St. James: 4. Pilgrims travelling to the grave of the saint. A malicious innkeeper slips a golden cup into a travelling bag. 5. The innkeeper denounces the pilgrim for theft, the cup is found, the son of the pilgrim sacrifices himself and is hanged. 6. The father finds his son, whom St. James has kept, still alive on the gallows. He returns to the inn with the judge. 7. The innkeeper claims that the hanged man is as dead as the chickens on his spit. But these fly away. 8. The hangman takes the fraudulent innkeeper to the gallows, and the young pilgrim is taken down and returns home with his father.

The townscape with the body of the saint is particularly interesting, as it is one of the oldest lifelike presentations of a German town, showing the market square of Rothenburg with the town hall as it looked before the fire in 1501.

The eastern end of the choir is formed by three precious glass paintings, 17 metres high, whose magnificent rich colouring comes into its own particularly impressively in the morning sun. The middle window (ca. 1350) shows scenes from the life and suffering of Christ, framed by the prophet. The right and left windows (both ca. 1400) portray the redemptive work of Jesus and the life of Mary.

Above the northern row of the choir stalls, we see the panels with coats of arms of Rothenburg patrician families who did great service as churchwardens. At the height of the steps, St. Michael bids up farewell from the choir area.

On the left next to the high altar, there is a large and richly structured tabernacle niche built into the side wall of the choir. The focal point of this many-figured work concerning the subject of

Transfer of the body of St. James to Santiago de Compostella

the Eucharist and altar sacrament is the presentation of the Trinity in the form of the so-called mercy seat above the actual niche (for storing the liturgical vessels). The very significant sculptural work dating from 1377 is unfortunately not completely preserved.

The first column of the nave bears four figures of the Apostles. The pulpit on the next column was installed in 1854. The outer wall features three memorial stones at the same height.

A holy bishop and an impressive Man of Sorrows flank the Wörnitzer- and Häutleinkapelle, while St. Matthew and St. Eustachius decorate the third column.

Richly structured tabernacle niche (1377) with the "palms" for paying for protection in church asylum

The new organ on the west gallery, consecrated in 1968, has been praised by experts from all over the world for its fullness of sound and the magnificent reproduction of the individual stops. It has two consoles with a total of 6 manuals, 69 ringing registers and 5,500 pipes. The numerous concerts given in the church are a delight for lovers of organ music.

Holy Blood Altar

Going up to the west choir, we can admire the most precious feature of the church: the Holy Blood Altar, one of the most important works of the famous sculptor and carver Tilman Riemenschneider (ca. 1460-1531).

This altar was created in 1500-04 on behalf of the Rothenburg Council in order to give a worthy setting to the Holy Blood relic venerated in the Middle Ages. The gold-plated cross (ca. 1270) is said to incorporate a rock crystal capsule with three drops of the blood of Jesus, giving the altar its name. The artistic altar backdrop was created in the workshop of the Rothenburg master Erhard Harschner.

Holy Blood Altar: Main section portraying the Last Supper with Judas in the centre handing bread to Christ

The impressive Last Supper scene vividly carved in lime-wood in the shrine unmistakably demonstrates Riemenschneider's great expressiveness as an artist. In the centre, highlighted and isolated from the others, stands Judas with the purse, handing Christ the morsel as he predicts: "One of you will betray me."

The Holy Blood Altar, Riemenschneider's masterpiece, featuring a golden cross with the famous relic set in an imposing filigree structure

Holy Blood Altar, scenes from the Mount of Olives and Christ's entry into Jerusalem

Depending on their temperament, the disciples react by showing dismay or helplessness or engaging in excited discussion. Only John remains impassive and trusting by the side of his Lord.

The bull's eye panes in the background accentuate the vivid impact of this masterpiece, as do the reliefs in the wings. These present the entry of Christ in Jerusalem and the Mount of Olives scenes with the disciples slumbering in the foreground, Jesus at prayer in the centre and in the background the bloodhounds entering the garden, led by the traitor Judas.

Feuerleinserker, with the Jakobskirche and gateway in the background

We leave the main church, turn right and enter Klingengasse, which goes through under the gallery of the church. There we come on the left to a pretty half-timbered house, the picturesque Feuerleinserker, with the Jakobskirche in the background, one of the most popular motifs in Rothenburg.

Favourite means of transport in Rothenburg

Wheel-lock rifle – south Germany, dated 1592

Guild chest of the bakers

Guild sign of the brewers

Decoration on cup of the Rothenburg Grocers' Association

Powder flask from the hunting ensemble of the French Queen Marie Antoinette, 1755-93

Imperial Town Museum

Opening hours:
April-Oct. daily 10 am–5 pm,
Nov.-March 1 pm–4 pm

INFORMATION

Klingentor

We leave the Imperial Town Museum and follow Klingengasse in a northerly direction towards the Klingentor, which used to be the fortification on the north-west corner of the town. The imposing gate tower with the high oriels is over 30 metres high. Like the other towers of the expanded town fortifications, the Strafturm, Galgentor, Rödertor and Kobolzeller Tor, the Klingentor dates from the end of the 14th c.

In the 16th c., a copper boiler was installed in the top of the tower as a water storage tank to supply numerous artesian wells in the town (e.g., Kappelplatzbrunnen). The spring water was fed through under the Tauber and pumped with water from the river via the pumping plant of the Bronnenmühle into the Klingenturm.

In front of this tower, a bastion was built around 1500 to strengthen the town fortifications, integrating St.-Wolfgangs-Kirche as part of the outer fortifications. On the outer wall of the church, we see embrasures instead of the church windows – there were also defensive positions behind the massive masonry.

On a tour, these battlements and the massive roof design and the cannon platforms as well as the old water pipes can still be seen. A drawbridge provided additional protection in front of the external gate tower with its half-timbered superstructure.

Klingengasse with Klingentor

The outer gate tower features the Shepherd's Dance Cabinet. St. Wolfgang was the patron saint of shepherds, and the shepherds' festival services used to be held here followed by celebrations and dancing. This is still recalled by the Shepherds' Dance performed several times a year.

Feuerleinserker (ca. 1600) – in Klingengasse

Klingenschütt on Schrannenplatz

**Farmers´ Museum
Klingengasse**

Opening hours: Daily Easter to October 31 st 10 am-6 pm, During Christmas market Sat., Sun. 10 am-5 pm

St.-Wolfgang´s or Shepherds´ Church

This Late Gothic fortress church was built from 1475 on a site where the shepherds used to say their prayers. St. Wolfgang was patron saint of their guild, supposed to preserve their herds against rapacious wolves. He is portrayed in a relief between the portals and the crucifix. The interior of the church can be discovered in a tour. The high altar structure depicts St. Wolfgang, flanked by St. Sebastian and St. Rochus. There are pictures from the legend of the three saints on the wings. Other features of the pleasing church interior are the Wendelin- and Marienaltar and the magnificent net vaults. The paintings on the wings of the high and Lady altar were created by the Rothenburg painter Wilhelm Ziegler in 1514-15.

St. Wolfgang's or Shepherds' Church: fortified church (15th c.) whose outer wall formed part of the town fortifications. Left, the outer gate tower of the Klingenbastei with the guardroom

A stone staircase in the massive north wall near the main altar leads to the vault-like military rooms under the church. The spiral staircase in the opposite corner leads up to the outer gate tower with the guardroom and to the battlements in the northern wall of the church.

St.-Wolfgangs-Kirche with late Gothic net vaults spanning the interior with its three altars

We leave St.-Wolfgangs-Kirche and turn right in front of the Klingentor. Past the Strafturm (prison tower), along the defensive wall and the former Dominican convent, we proceed through a side gate into the site of the former castle complex, today called Burggarten.

St.-Wolfgangs-Kirche

Opening hours:
April-Sept. 11 am-1 pm and 2 pm-5pm, Oct. 11 am-1 pm and 2 pm-4 pm, Tuesdays closed

12 Burgtor

The Burgtor is the largest and oldest gate tower in Rothenburg (12th c.). From the middle gate house, a drawbridge once led over the moat into the castle site. The front gate decorated with town, Habsburg and Hohenstaufen coats of arms with the two little guard and customs houses was added only after 1460. The inner wooden gate is dated 1555. At night, only the small entrance in the large gate was opened in order to prevent raids.

Burgtor: Largest and oldest gate tower of Rothenburg (14th c.). The front gate with little guard and customs houses dates from the 16th c.

L.: The massive Strafturm on the north-west flank of the town wall

13 *In the Burggarten*

The origin of Rothenburg is to be sought on this promontory projecting into the valley of the Tauber, today a well-kept park offering magnificent views. The old Frankish castle of the counts of Rothenburg, probably begun in the 10th c., first stood here.

After the line of the counts died out, the Hohenstaufens expanded the castle and built an even larger complex, the Reichsburg, in the front part of the present Burggarten. With the settlement of craftsmen and servants, a growing municipality was created under its protection in the 12th-14th c. Rothenburg became a free imperial town in 1274.

At the beginning of the 15th c., there was a total population of about 20,000 in the town and almost 170 surrounding villages covering approx. 400 sq. km. From the natural lookout terrace, we can look far down into the valley of the Tauber with its numerous mills, some of which still operate today, and the old hamlet Detwang.

View from the Burggarten of the southern part of Rothenburg

Beautiful show of flowers in the Burggarten

The rise opposite the promontory is called Engelsburg because a Celtic rampart (refuge) was thrown up there about 2,000 years ago. This offered probably the most comprehensive view over the entire medieval town, and it was here that the famous etcher Merian (1593-1650) made his portrait of Rothenburg.

We see on the left the western town fortifications up to the Klingentor and on the right up to the Stöberleinsturm in the "Kappenzipfel".

Blasiuskapelle

Only one building of the Reichsburg partially withstood the earthquake of 1356: the Blasiuskapelle, also called the "High House of the Dukes", which has remained preserved. The murals of the Hohenstaufen chapel date from the time of the reconstruction around 1400. Today the chapel serves as a memorial commemorating the dead of the two world wars, and a memorial stone in front recalls the Jewish community. The giant ashlars are the last remains of the castle architecture in Rothenburg's High Romanesque-Hohenstaufen era. The citizens used the stone of the other buildings to build their houses and defensive works.

We leave the Blasiuskapelle and return in the direction of the Burgtor.

The partially Romanesque Blasiuskapelle

15

Herrngasse

We proceed through the Burgtor back into the town. The first building on the left is the very famous puppet theatre, Köhler's Figurentheater für Erwachsene (Puppet Theatre

Herrngasse: Proud patrician houses line Rothenburg's widest lane. Herrnbrunnen is in the foreground.

for Adults).

Herrngasse, lined by proud patrician houses, forms a link between the Burggarten and the town hall. It is also called Herrnmarkt, where the horse and cattle market, a privilege of the patricians, used to be held.

Figurentheater am Burgtor

Opening hours:
June-Sept. daily 3 pm-8 pm,
Sun. closed; Oct.-April daily
8 pm, Sat. 3 pm and 8 pm, Sun. closed

Every gable is different. A beam, which facilitated the hauling up of goods, projects over the warehouse hatches. In times of need and war, every household had to "store" a prescribed amount of food and other necessities. Inscriptions on panels document that emperors and kings stayed the night in these venerable buildings.

Romantic inner court of the Staudt patrician house with galleries over several floors

The Herrnbrunnen in the middle of the lane dates from 1595. Because of its high location above the Tauber, Rothenburg built numerous wells. The location of the supply pipes from outside was kept a strict secret and known only to the mayor and the council of the town. That was important because the enemy could cut off or poison the water supply during a siege.

The houses No. 11 and 15 have retained their romantic inner courts, as has the Staudt House with its artistically designed lattices opposite. This accommodated the Emperors Karl V and Ferdinand I, Queen Eleonore of Sweden and the wife of Gustav Adolph. The attractive inner courtyard with galleries, oriel and stairway tower is probably the most beautiful in Rothenburg. A massive spiral-shaped wooden staircase links the floors in the interior of the building, which is still lived in by the von Staudt family. Portraits of ancestors from four centuries uphold the tradition of the old patrician family.

Staudt patrician house

Opening hours: Please consult Gunther and Christian von Staudt Tel: 0 98 61/9 29 42

16 Franziskanerkirche

The High Gothic Franciscan church on the other side of the
street belonged to the monastery of the begging order,
founded in 1281. The simple basilica was consecrated in
1309. A wooden breasting, or rood screen, separates the
choir area, formerly seat of the monks, from the nave, the

Franciscan church with Franciscan altar by Tilman Riemenschneider

area for the lay congregation.

The pictures (which have become partially unrecognizable)
on this show Christ's way of the cross and hail from the 14th
c. The floor and the walls of the church feature numerous

Interior of Franciscan church, the oldest church in Rothenburg (consecrated in 1309), view of rood screen

gravestones and bronze coats of arms of Rothenburg patrician families and the neighbouring landed gentry.

Dietrich von Berlichingen, grandfather of the famous Götz, was also buried here.

The grave of Hans von Beulendorf and his wife Margreth on the northern pillar in front of the rood screen is particularly noteworthy.

The artistic Franciscan altar with a portrayal of the stigmatisation of St. Francis of Assisi – a work by Riemenschneider – is also presented in the church. The adjoining monastery buildings now accommodate the Goethe Institute, which offers foreigners instruction in German.

Today, the Goethe Institute is also an international cultural and assembly centre that stages numerous events.

Franciscan altar by Tilman Riemenschneider (1490) depicting St. Francis and his fellow brother Leo during the mystic revelation of Christ

Doll & Toy Museum

At Herterichsbrunnen, the picturesque Hofbronnengasse takes us to the Doll & Toy Museum. Very close to the market, only a few steps from the market square down into the valley past Georgsbrunnen, is the beginning of Hofbronnengasse, where the Hofbronnen, which gave the lane its name, is a little hidden to the right.

The second and third house in Hofbronnengasse 11-13 accommodates one of the most attractive toy museums in Europe.

From left: Hofbronnen in Hofbronnengasse. Little antique shop (ca. 1920)
3 character dolls – standing: Schildkröt Series No. 727,
Sitting l.: Character doll of SFBJ, Paris,
seated to the r.: Character doll from Krämer & Rheinhard series 126.
Interior palace hall Petit Trianon.

Doll & Toy Museum

Hofbronnengasse 11–13
Telefon: 0 98 61/ 73 30

Opening hours:
Daily 9.30 am-6 pm, Jan. and Feb. 11 am-5 pm

It's worthwhile taking a little time to let yourself be carried away into the dream world of childhood in the past. The private toy museum, founded in 1984, is accommodated in two houses from the 15th and 17th c. that are protected as historic monuments.

The museum lovingly presents two hundred years of toy history with well over 1,000 dolls from German, French non-European manufactories exhibited in lively scenes. The many accessories enhancing these are noteworthy features. The doll's rooms, kitchens and shops as well wonderfully enchanting doll's houses show how our ancestors used to live.

And the museum also presents tin toys, railways, theatre, farms, circus, merry-go-rounds, lively fair scenes, hand-carved wooden toys as well as thousands of lovely miniature toys from a children's world long since past, "a cultural history in miniature".

Special exhibitions on various subjects are held continually over the year. Visiting this museum is certainly to be recommended.

There is another museum located only few metres away from the Doll & Toy Museum down the valley: the Medieval Crime Museum.

Medieval Crime Museum

This museum is the only legal museum in Europe with the most important collection on legal history anywhere. It displays a unique and comprehensive overview of the over 1,000-year-old legal history on four floors on 2,000 sq.m. and in over 130 cabinets. The museum presents the development of legislation up to the 19th c., as well as the medieval criminal procedure, gruesome instruments of torture and corporal punishment, along with devices for carrying out

Public punishments in the Middle Ages

degrading punishments, the neck-violas for cantankerous women, shame-masks or the pillory – some of which we certainly find amusing. The history of the law is, of course, connected with documents and the seals necessary for their legal effectiveness, and many of the documents exhibited are elaborately designed. A great deal of space in the museum is given to the copperplate engravings and woodcuts of sensational criminal cases.

Dipping apparatus for punishing bakers for baking loaves that were too small or too large

The police regulations show how even the most private areas of life were regimented by clothing, marriage or baptismal regulations. It is worth noting the coins and medals to commemorate legislation or famous legal cases, the legal symbolism, colloquial idioms that have their origin in law and the caricatures of the judicial system and administration. The houses and walls of the town certainly show visitors the setting in which our ancestors lived, but say little about the legal conditions that governed them. The Medieval Criminal Museum gives us the appropriate information.

Left:
Iron Maiden, iron-mounted
stigmatizing and punishment
coat for women and girls (16th c.),
studded with nails on the inside

Right: Pillory scene

1. Rosary, punishment for neglectful or sleeping churchgoers – 2. Shame-mask for women, tongue and ears indicating addiction to gossip – 3. Instrument for breaking offenders on the wheel – 4. Spiky chair, instrument of torture from the time of the witch trials – 5. Neck-violas for bad girls and women, below double neck-viola for two quarrelsome women – 6. Executioner's mask – 7. Handcuffs with finger screw – 8. Madhouse – 9. Chastity belt,

guaranteeing marital fidelity – 10. Iron collar with handcuffs and chain – 11. Baker's chair for dipping into water as punishment for baking undersize loaves – 12. Shame-mask for evil women – 13. Drinker's barrel for notorious pub patrons – 14. Shame-flute for bad musicians – 15. Interrogation table with finger screws

19 Johanniskirche

We're only a few metres from the Gothic Johanniskirche. On its completion (ca. 1400), parts of the oldest town fortification were included in the masonry. On the gable side, we notice one of the door hinges for the former town gate, the Johannistor, which had become superfluous after the first town expansion.

Fountain near Johanniskirche

Plönlein and Siebersturm

Coming from the Johanniskirche, we proceed into Untere Schmiedgasse to the right and shortly afterwards stand on the famous Plönlein (original "Plönlein" = small square).

The road junction opens up one of the most attractive town-scapes in Germany with the pic-turesque half-timbered house with the fountain in front flan-ked by the Siebersturm and Kobolzeller Tor. Half-timbered gables and wrought-iron inn signs frame this harmonious com-position.

Plönlein, one of the most beautiful medieval town motifs in Germany

The Siebersturm in Spitalgasse is fortified on the outer side with defiant giant ashlars. The Jo-hannitertor formed the southern entrance to Rothenburg in the 12th c.

However, after more and more craftsmen had settled on the edge of the flourishing town, efforts were made as early as 1204 to include the new residen-tial districts within the protection of the fortifications.

There was also expansion to the south by some hundred metres, the conclusion being formed by the Siebersturm and Kobolzeller Tor towards the Tauber valley.

Siebersturm (13th c.), seen from the hospital quarter ("Kappenzipfel"), fortified tower to the south before the second town extension

Weißer Turm

Kobolzeller Tor

Klingenturm

Galgentor

Röderturm
Alte Schmiede

Siebersturm

Markusturm
Röderbogen

Burgtor

In the inner courtyard of Kobolzeller Tor

Kobolzeller Tor: The outer gate displays coat of arms of the free imperial town (imperial eagle) and town coats of arms

The fortifications of Kobolzeller Tor secured the way up via the "Steige" from the Tauber valley. Through the inner gate tower, we come into the rectangular bastion with the "Teufelskanzel" ("Devil's Pulpit") as look-out surrounded by merlons. The outer gate decorated with coats of arms is additionally protected by the Kohlturm next to it and surrounds the outer ward. Because of the steep site, the architects had not dared to build the tower over the entrance, as otherwise usual. In the outer ward area, there are still prayer stations of the stations of the cross from the former pilgrimage path up into the town .

If we take some steps down the street, we gain an attractive view of this massive bulwark and the Siebersturm in the background.

Rossmühle

The way above the bastion leads us to the Rossmühle, a squat building with supporting buttresses. If supplies of flour from the numerous mills in the Tauber valley were interrupted in times of war or there was a lack of water, 16 horses were harnessed here within the town walls to circle around to turn four millstones via a gin. On the rear side of the present youth hostel, we find the remains of a lime tree of 1587.

Rossmühle, formerly with four millstones driven by 16 horses, today a youth hostel

In this area, the roofed-over battlements are accessible on foot as far as Kobolzeller Tor, the only still accessible section towards the Tauber valley. At the Rossmühle, on the battlements a double-seated toilet can still be seen through a small door opening.

Youth hostel dining hall

Hegereiterhaus and Spitalhof

We go on to the Spitalhof, dominated by the original Hegereiterhaus in its centre. With its pointed tented roof and the round stairway tower with the dainty lamp, this forms an attractive contrast to the almost sober functional surrounding buildings. This was built by the architect Weidmann, as was the main building.

Hegereiterhaus – home for the suppliers of the hospital goods (1591)

The large hospital kitchen was set up in the basement, while the upper floor served as apartment for the suppliers of the numerous hospital goods. The main building with the gable side to the street accommodated the hospital administration of the Order of he Holy Ghost until the Reformation and then the hospital until 1948. Today the buildings are used as an old people's home. Behind the artistic wrought-iron railings on the north side is the well installation in the former cellar and bakery, which was renovated and now serves as a youth hostel. It is adjoined on the left by the "plague house" with its isolation cells.

24 Stöberleinsturm

The Stöberleinsturm, steeped in legend with its picturesque corner oriels, has an almost dainty appearance. The hospital complex "Zum Heiligen Geist" was created from 1280, when the town built a hospital outside the walls, as was usual at

Stöberleinsturm, steeped in legend

that time. Thanks to several foundations at the beginning and numerous gifts in subsequent centuries, the members of the order were able to care adequately for the sick and poor. They also administered the hospital goods and – until the building was included in the town fortifications – provided overnight accommodation for travellers who had not been admitted into the town because of the onset of darkness.

25 Die Spitalkirche

The foundation stone for the Gothic hospital church was laid as early as 1281.

Main altar of the hospital church, crucifix with Mary and John

The precious elements of the altar assembled in 1953 date from the first half of the 15th c.: a wooden crucifix, flanked by the stone figures of John and Mary.

One of the gravestones behind the altar commemorates Count Otto von Flügelau (d. 1317), one of the founders of the church.

The presentation of Mary on the right side of the choir dates about from the same time.

Figure of the Virgin Mary, 14th c.

Hospital church (from 1281): on the right of the main altar the pulpit, l. the baptismal stone and tabernacle

The tabernacle opposite (ca. 1390) shows to the right and left of the door the Annunciation scene with Mary and the Angel Gabriel. Over the door sways the Christ child on a rainbow, the bridge between God and man, to Mary. However, Christ stands over all. The niche used to serve for keeping the sacramental wine and the Hosts.

Tabernacle ca. 1390-1400. Restored inscription "Anno Domini 1625" above older inscription; above, Man of Sorrows

Imperial town hall

The spacious hospital district is completed by the massive "Zehntscheune" (warehouse for a tenth of the harvest) dating from 1699. In 1975, the European year for the protection of historic monuments, it was converted into a modern conference venue, the present imperial town hall. It can cater for as many as 150-500 persons or – with seats in rows – accommodate 600 persons in an historic setting. We now leave the area of the Heilig-Geist-Spital on the southeast corner and proceed to the southern town gate.

Hospital bastion: Sturdiest bulwark of the town fortifications (16th c.) with seven gates, portcullises, drawbridge and passable terreplein

Spitalbastei / Faulturm

This is Rothenburg's most recent fortification, completed in the 16th c. by Leonhard Weidmann. The two bastions set one behind the other are in the shape of an eight. Seven gates, most of them secured with portcullises, the drawbridge at the entrance and the terreplein passable by guns above the defiant giant

Cannon platform with old cannons

ashlars made the hospital bastion Rothenburg's mightiest bulwark. The inscription in the keystone of the external archway: "Pax intrantibus, Salus exeuntibus" ("Peace to those entering, hail to those departing") only appears to contrast with this.

Outer view of the Spitalbastei

The terreplein was very recently restored and opened for visitors. The adventure playground in the moat offers children and their accompanying adults an opportunity to relax a little after spending hours taking in the historic sights.

Faulturm

At the gate tower of the Spitalbastei, we go on the battlements, past the massive "Faulturm". According to legend, the tower is as deep as it is high, its lower part serving as "Hungerturm", where the remains of the criminals rotted.

The town wall with the impressive "Faulturm", from where it was possible to observe the area between Röder- and Spitalbastei.

Old Forge and battlements

The stroll over the town wall provides views over the embrasures and glimpses of back yards and little gardens full of nooks and crannies. The houses built close to one another and nestling up to the town wall show how little space there was available within the protecting wall.

View from the Röderturm of the town wall with battlements

Romantic half-timbered gables on the town wall with the battlements. In the background the Röderturm and Old Forge in front on the left.

Soon we pass a steep half-timbered gable of the attractive "Old Forge". The name plates between the embrasures specify donors who contributed to the reconstruction and preservation of the town wall after the second world war.

Roofed-over battlements and town wall

Old Forge

Today Rothenburg again seeks donors who wish to contribute something towards preserving the town wall. The town administration honours these persons with plaques bearing their names affixed at the section of the wall that has been restored with their donations.

At the following the gate tower, the Rödertor, we descend from the battlements and proceed around the bastion. The battlements here are strengthened with a parallel "outer ward".

Rödertor: Bastion with double moat, three archways and outer ward in front of the main gate. There are little customs and guard houses in front.

The main gate was protected in 1615 by a bastion with twin ditch, drawbridge and three gate arches. As for the Burgtor, there are two little guard and customs houses on the outside in front.

The main tower can be climbed up and provides a magnificent view over the maze of roofs and the invariably lively lanes of the old town.

View from Röderturm over the roofs of the town looking towards Jakobskirche

View from Röderturm to the south into the hospital quarter, the "Kappenzipfel"

Röderturm

Opening hours:
Daily depending on the weather
9 am-6 pm, Dec.-Feb. closed,
except for Christmas Market

Markusturm and Röderbogen

Passing through Rödergasse into the town, we come to the Markusturm, which with the Röderbogen is also part of the oldest town fortifications. We can still identify the contours of the original battlements under the steep hip roof installed at later date. The Büttelhaus behind the Röderbogen, which was used as a prison up into the 18th c., now accommodates the town archive. The Röderbogen with its lance-like tower superstructure and the massive Markusturm along with the simple Renaissance fountain and the vine-covered half-timbered houses of Rödergasse provide one of the most attractive scenes in Rothenburg.

If you still have some energy left, you should turn in front of the Röderbogen to the left into the old town ditch to see the "Old Rothenburg Craftsmen's House, No. 26".

Markusturm with Röderbogen and Büttelhaus

Old Rothenburg Craftmen´s House

This house, built between 1270 and 1300, accommodated all manner of craftsmen over seven centuries. It was successively lived in by coopers, dyers of black fabrics, weavers, shoemakers, tinkers, potters, basket makers, soap-boilers, pavers, tinsmiths and masons. The preservation of this gem is due above all to a recluse who left his long-standing residence in its original state in the modern age because he did not need either running water or electricity.

Old Rothenburg Craftsmen's House – shoemakers' workshop

Old Rothenburg Craftsmen´s House
Alter Stadtgraben 26

Opening hours:
April -Oct. daily 9 am-6 pm.
Nov. and Dec. Mon-Fr. 2 pm-4 pm
Sat., Sun. 10 am-4 pm. Jan.-March closed

Parents' bedroom in Old Rothenburg Craftsmen's House

The well in the interior, 14 metres deep, could also supply water today. The low ceilings and doorways and the dimensions of the beds are a reminder that our ancestors were much smaller than we are.

The building has eleven rooms and small rooms with the original furnishings, one of the most interesting being the kitchen with its open fireplace. The uneven tiles on the oven in the living room were turned on a potter's wheel in the 14th c.

Patrician kitchen with fireplace for cooking

Passing through the Röderbogen, we enter the oldest area of Rothenburg. Along the front of the Büttelhaus, we follow the line of the first town wall via the Milchmarkt to Kapellenplatz with the Seelbrunnen. A little further on, we see on the right the Weisser Turm, one of the few remains of the oldest inner town fortifications from the 12th c. and the adjoining half-timbered building is the Jewish Dancing House, which also served as inn. This was bordered by the quarter of the second Jewish community, which was expelled from the town in 1520.

Judengasse, as interconnected and still preserved residential area of the former Jewish community, is with its excavations and finds particularly interesting for Jewish history in the free imperial towns. The Jewish Dancing House was later used a hostel for the poor or "Seelhaus". The Renaissance foun-

Seelbrunnen at Kapellenplatz (1626)

tain on the neighbouring Kapellenplatz is still called "Seelbrunnen" after this.

The square in turn owes its name to a Lady Chapel, which served as the synagogue of the Rothenburg Jews up to the end of the 14th c. and was demolished in 1804-05. The original Jewish quarter with its about 500 inhabitants was also around Kapellenplatz until it was moved to the new Judengasse outside the inner wall.

L.: Weisser Turm, part of the oldest town fortifications (12th c.). The half-timbered facade of the Jewish Dancing House adjoins this on the left.

33 Galgentor

Galgengasse used to lead to the gallows outside the town. It was the visible sign of the legal sovereignty of the free imperial town and was demolished after this was lost in 1810. The Galgentor or Würzburger Tor was the most frequently contested entrance to Rothenburg. Tilly's and Turènes' troops also entered the town here during the Thirty Years' War. Only the defiant gate tower and one of the front towers have remained of the fortifications. The moat, rampart and the two defensive towers have meanwhile been restored.

The Galgentor marks the end of the historic army march, which leads out of the town to the festival ground every Whitsun. In front of the tower, the participants in the parade pitch their camp, which up into the early evening hours provides a colourful picture of soldiers' life from the time of the Thirty Years' War. The very recently exposed secret escape route at the former bastion is opened to the public at this time.

The town has created an adventure playground in the moat of the town, as at Spitaltor.

Würzburger Tor or Galgentor with front gate and two defensive towers, as well as moat and rampart

Twin bridge and Kobolzeller Kirchlein

The Kobolzeller Kirchlein and twin bridge are located outside the fortifications, direct on the Tauber.

Kobolzeller Kirchlein, also called church "Zu unserer lieben Frau" ("To Our Blessed Lady")

The medieval fortified town of Rothenburg with its towers rises above the Tauber valley with the Bogenbrücke (1330) and Kobolzeller Kirchlein.

The peculiar twin bridge dating from 1330 – once protected with a tower – provided further protection for Kobolzeller Tor. From the other bank, there are many motifs with the bridge and Kobolzeller Kirchlein in the foreground and the silhouette of the well-fortified town with all its towers above.

l.: St. Christopher (1480-90)
r.: St. John the Baptist (ca. 1520)

The Late Gothic church (15th c.) lost most of its art treasures during the Peasants' War. Millers incited by the iconoclast Dr. Karlstadt plundered the church on Easter Monday 1525, destroyed the works and threw the remains into the river. The old pilgrims' church can still be viewed in May after prayers. Pilgrims' churches with their altars served as prayer stations for the St. James pilgrims. The pilgrims could use a twin spiral staircase turning around itself leading up to station on the west gallery.

Hall church with view of stone people's altar

36 Das Topplerschlösschen

Passing over the twin bridge, we reach after a short walk a curiously castle-like building, a residential tower, the Topplerschlösschen, built in 1388 for Mayor Heinrich Toppler. Modelled on the over 1,000 year-old little aristocrat's lodge, it served Toppler as summer seat and venue for discussions with important political personalities. King Wenzel is said to have also been a frequent guest of Toppler here.

Topplerschlösschen, built in the Tauber valley in the 14th c. for Mayor Toppler

Kitchen with fireplace

The great mayor, sometimes even called "King of Rothenburg", had made the land round about safe, and it may be assumed that he wanted to demonstrate this with the building outside the town wall. The little moated castle decorated with coats of arms recalls a Romanesque tower with a residential section, as had been very usual over two hundred years previously. Today the inner rooms are still furnished as at the time of the builder, but with furniture from very many stylistic eras (16th -19th c.). They can be viewed all year round.

Topplerschlösschen: Sitting room of Rothenburg's greatest mayor

**Topplerschlösschen
in the Tauber valley**

**Opening hours:
Entire year Fr., Sat., 1 pm-4 pm
Closed in November**

Parish church in Detwang

A half-hour walk through Klingentor or along the north-west town wall brings us into the Tauber valley and to the hamlet Detwang.
Detwang's St. Peter and Paul parish church was consecrated as early as 968, making it one of the oldest fortified churches in Franconia.

Romanesque St. Peter and Paul parish church (consecrated in 968)

Detwang parish church

Opening hours:
April-Oct. 8.30 am-12 am and
1.30 pm-5 pm (from 1.6-14.9 until 6 pm).
Nov.-march
10 am-12 am and 2 pm-4 pm. Monday closed

Northern side altar (ca. 1480-90). In the shrine on the left the monk Anthony, in the centre St. Katharina (figure ca. 1440) and on the right St. Nicholas. The altar pictures are of St. Stephan (l.) and St. Laurentius.

Southern side altar (ca. 1500-10). In the shrine on the left St. Ottilie, in the middle "moon sickle" Madonna with the child Jesus and apple, the sign of redemption, and on the right a saint in nun's habit. The altar pictures show St. Barbara (l.) and St. Magdalena.

Holy Cross Altar: In the left side altar, Jesus in the Garden of Gethsemane; in the centre, the crucifixion with the mourning women and a group of mercenaries; in the right side wing, the resurrected Christ with flag of victory.

The church's main attraction, however, is its main altar, the cross altar by Tilman Riemenschneider, crafted around 1510 originally for the Michaelskapelle in Rothenburg. The altar was moved from this church, which was badly damaged in the Thirty Years' War, to Detwang.

The wing reliefs with the Mount of Olives scene and presentation of the resurrection of Christ were created by assistants, while the main group is the work of the master. Sadness and sympathy are impressively shown in the faces of the Mary group with John and the mercenaries.

Painted baptismal font (1720)

Historic festivals and events

(For dates, see event calendar)

The "Master Draught"

This festival has been held every Whitsun since 1881, the story of the legend being played by local amateur actors before tens of thousands of guests, recently also on the second Saturday in July (Summer Festival) and in September (Imperial Town Festival).

Historic festival: Tilly with commander's baton

The legend describes the wondrous rescue of Rothenburg on October 31st 1631 – during the Thirty Years' War. Enraged at the violent resistance put up by the town, Tilly wanted to have four of the councillors executed. All pleas for mercy came to naught, and Mayor Bezold had to fetch the hangman.

Meanwhile Tilly was offered the finest Franconian wine in an enormous tankard, holding 3 1/4 litres. He promised to spare the town if one of the councillors drained the cup at one draught.

The former mayor Nusch accepted the challenge and performed the feat, and the astonished Tilly kept his promise, to the jubilation of the population.

The former mayor Nusch draining the elector's tankard of 1616, once probably the welcoming tankard of the imperial town. The huge drinking vessel (holding 3 1/4 litres) is associated with the legend of the "Master Draught". It is exhibited in the Imperial Town Museum.

Hans Sachs Festival

Hans Sachs (1494-1576), a trained shoemaker, lived in Nuremberg as a "Meistersinger" and made a name for himself as "shoemaker's poet". He wrote countless verses as well as 208 plays. Since 1921, a Rothenburg company of players has performed some of his finest merry tales in the Kaisersaal of the town hall every Easter and Whitsun, in the summer months May to August and during the Imperial Town Festival.

Apart from this historic setting, the festival is given its special character by the costumes and music from the Meistersinger era.

Easter programme

Over Easter, Rothenburg presents to its visitors the historic Shepherds' Dance, a presentation of the Hans Sachs Festival as well as Easter concerts on the market square and an organ concert. The Figurentheater für Erwachsene (Puppet Theatre for Adults) at the Burgtor also puts on performances.

Whitsun programme

Amateur actors perform the historic festival "The Master Draught" in the Kaisersaal of the town hall twice on Saturday, Sunday and Monday.

The "Historic Shepherds' Dance" takes place on the market square on Whit Sunday. The programme also includes the Hans Sachs Festival and Puppet Theatre for Adults as well as concerts in St.-Jakobs-Kirche and in the open air. On the Monday, visitors feel taken back to the time of the Thirty Years' War. In the early morning, soldiers in medieval garb move through the old town. In the afternoon (from 3 pm), the "historic army on the march in 1631" proceeds from Spitaltor through Spital-gasse, Schmiedgasse and Galgengasse to Galgentor, where it encamps. After the end of the event towards 7 pm, Tilly takes the parade of the troops marching past on the town hall square.

Summer Festival in Rothenburg

The summer festivities are held on the second weekend in July. They are opened by a citizens' festival in Burggarten on Saturday afternoon offering entertainment until into the evening. The historic festival "The Master Draught" and the Shepherds' Dance are also presented on Saturday. The weekend ends enchantingly with an evening serenade in the festively illuminated Burggarten, the "Night of the 1,000 Candles".

Imperial Town Festival

The second weekend in September is again devoted to the history of Rothenburg. It begins with a torchlight procession of those taking part in the Historical Festival, moving from the Taubergrund to the market square on Friday evening.

On Saturday afternoon, the people of Rothenburg perform for their guests historic scenes from seven centuries in the lanes and on the squares of the old town. The big fireworks display with the illumination of the town in the evening recalls the bombardments of Rothenburg in days gone by. The Historical Festival continues for the whole of Sunday. "The Master Draught" and the historic Shepherds' Dance are also presented.

Above:
Rothenburg militia

Left:
Transport of prisoners

Below left:
Cellarman

Below right:
Mercenaries

Historic Shepherds' Dance

Every year, the "Shepherds' Guild" meets for its historic dances in front of the town hall in the afternoon on Easter and Whit Sunday as well as on the second Saturday in July and September. Already in Middle Ages, the shepherds danced around the Herterichsbrunnen on the southern side of the town hall.

Legend has it that with their dance the shepherds once prevented the plague breaking out in Rothenburg. According to another legend, a local shepherd discovered a treasure in a wondrous dream that made the shepherds dance for joy.

Historic Shepherds' Dance: "The Shepherds' Guild" dances on the market square in front of the town hall

Herrgottskirche in Creglingen

From Detwang, we proceed 18 km down the Tauber to the old hamlet of Creglingen.

The Gothic Herrgottskirche (1380) is located about 1.5 km on the left in a side valley. It was built by the counts of Hohenlohe-Brauneck as a depository and place of veneration for a Host found here during ploughing.

Herrgottskirche Creglingen: Lady altar, a masterpiece by the carver Tilman Riemenschneider

Riemenschneider's famous Lady altar – also known as Creglinger Altar – formed the monumental monstrance for this from about 1510. Other noteworthy works of art from that time are four more altars as well as artistic wooden carvings (possibly by Veit Stoss) on the choir stalls and the crucifix.

Winter fairy tale in Rothenburg

Rothenburg offers its guests an attractive programme from the beginning of December to January 6th, featuring contemplative, historic and romantic, but also cheerfully entertaining events, Christmas serenades, choir and organ concerts, chamber concerts, songs sung by children and children's theatre, performances by the Rothenburg Epiphany Carol Singers and Christmas evenings in the hotels with musical accompaniment, delighting music lovers in particular.

Events also include a torchlight procession of the school children, rambles by torchlight, walks through the woods (with rest stops for mulled wine), mail coach trips for children as well as town and museum tours. Other constant attractions during these weeks are the Christmas crib at the town hall, the art exhibition, Hans Sachs Festival and the puppet theatre as well as the Old Rothenburg Christmas Market (until shortly before Christmas). New Year's Eve balls in the hotels and restaurants complete the attractive programme.

1 Market square
2 Town hall
3 Herterichsbrunnen
4 Baumeisterhaus
5 Art exhibition in Meat and Dancing House
6 Historical Vaults
7 Old Grammar School
8 Jakobskirche
9 Imperial town museum
10 Klingentor
11 St. Wolfgangskirche/ Country Museum
12 Burgtor
13 Burggarten
14 Blasiuskapelle
15 Herrngasse
16 Franziskanerkirche
17 Doll & Toy Museum
18 Medieval Crime Museum
19 St.-Johannis-Kirche
20 Plönlein, Siebersturm
21 Kobolzeller Tor
22 Rossmühle
23 Hegereiterhaus

Tour of the main sights

Information

 toilets

P Parking space

☎ Telephone

▲ Way up to town wall

This tour follows the course of the first town wall. From Judengasse via 32 and 30 through the old town moat to Johanniskirche 19.

Burggarten (5 minutes from town hall square; illuminated from nightfall)

Burggarten – Taubertal – Kobolzeller Kirchlein (church) – Twin Bridge– Kobolzeller Tor

Burggarten – Topplerschlösschen – Fuchsmühle – Barbarossa bridge

Footpath in direction of Strafturm
Topplerschlösschen – Engelsburg
Klosterweg – Taubertal – Detwang

The marked circular paths starting from the town require close on 2 hours to cover:

Magpie:
Spitaltor – Schandtaubertal – Blinktal – Kobolzeller Tor

Kite:
Spitaltor – Taubertal – Natursteig – Spitaltor

Fox:
Kobolzellertor – Twin bridge – Engelsburg – Klingentor

Water wagtail:
Galgentor – Steffeleinsbrunnen – Steinbachtal – Klingentor

Hare:
Galgentor – Steffeleinsbrunnen – Steinbachtal – Bettwar – Klingentor

Guided theme hikes have been offered for some years. Details of dates can be obtained from the Information Office at the market square.

Theme hikes include:
Mill hikes
Music hikes
Vineyard hikes

The World Walking Day is also an established part of the Rothenburg event calendar.

Index

Tips and addresses

Emergency services
Police (accident, assault)
Tel. 1 10
Fire: Tel. 1 12
First aid:
Ambulance – Bayer. Red Cross,
Tel: 1 92 22

Information, accommodation, events
Kultur- und Fremdenverkehrsamt,
D-91541 Rothenburg ob der Tauber,
Marktplatz 2 (Town councillors´
tavern), Tel: (0 98 61) 4 04-8 00,
P.O. Box 1114, Telex: 61379 roti d,
Fax: 86807

Fishing
District Fishing Club
Tel: 32 89 (Mr. Schmid)

Library, reading room:
Klingengasse 6, Tel. 4 04-54,
Closed Wed.

Railways information
Station, Tel: 1 94 19

Camping sites
Tauberidyll, Detwang, Tel: 31 77
and Tauberromantik, Detwang,
Tel: 61 91

Cycle hire
Rothenburg station, Tel: 23 30

Telephone services
Trunk dialling code: 0 98 61,
Information (inland): 1 18 33,
Information (abroad): 1 18 34,
Telegram acceptance: 01 13,
Phone boxes:
see street map (page 114/115)

Airfield, sight-seeing flights
Aero-Club, Bauerngraben,
tel. 74 74

Frankenfreizeit:
Indoor ozone swimming pool
(mid-September to mid-May) and
heated open-air swimming pool
(mid-May to mid-September),
Tel: 45 65; sauna and massages,
Tel: 56 66, restaurant with large
terrace, Tel: 39 71, Nördlinger
Strasse (Romantic Road)

Guided tours
May-Oct., Dec. daily 11 am and 2 pm,
April daily 2 pm, from 10 persons,
9.30 pm market square. Guided
tours through the illuminated old
town. With suitable weather daily,
from 10 persons

Lost property office
Town hall arcades, entrance far left,
Tel: 4 04-56

Changing money
At all banks and savings banks, in
travel agents and market square
and Hotel Tilman Riemenschneider,
Georgengasse 11-13

Golf links
Colmberg Palace; 18 km,
Tel: (0 98 03) 2 62

Church services
Catholic: Sunday 7, 8.30., 10.30 St.
Johanniskirche, Protestant: Sunday
7, 9 St. Jakobskirche

Group activities
Tours of the town day and night,
welcome by the historic cellarman,
meeting with historic night watchman, walk over Engelsburg to
Detwang, tour guide, special performances of the Hans Sachs Festival
and the doll theatres, dance music,
Hans Sachs music, organ concert,
information at Tourist Office see
above

Indoor swimming pools
see Frankenfreizeit

Youth hostels
Rossmühle, Mühlacker 1,
Tel: 9 41 60, Fax: 94 16 20;
Spitalhof, Tel: 78 89

Children´s playgrounds
With adventure playgrounds in the
moats at Würzburger Tor and at
Spitaltor; at the indoor swimming
pool, Nördlinger Strasse

Kneipp water-treading facility
At „Riviera" path

Hospital
Ansbacher Str. 131,
Tel: 70 70 and 7 07 25

Coach rides
Tour of the town, half- and whole-
day excursions, information from
Tourist Office

Museums
Imperial town museum, Medieval
Crime Museum, Old Rothenburg
Craftsmen's House, Topplerschlöss-
chen, Historical Vaults, Doll & Toy
Museum, Country Museum. Details
of opening hours are given in this
guide.

Police
Tel: 97 10
(Motorway police Tel: 97 12 61)

Post offices
Milchmarkt 5,
Bahnhofstr. 7,
Rückertstr. 4

Imperial town hall
Large hall up to 600 seats,
Small hall, parking area, Spitalhof,
Tel: 48 66

Travel agents
Marktplatz 2 (Town councillors'
tavern), Tel: 46 11

Riding
Riding stall Schwanensee (3 km),
Tel: 32 62

Benches
Paths around the old town, in the
Burggarten, on the "Tauber Riviera"

Sauna:
see Frankenfreizeit

Shooting
Small bore, air rifle, pistols,
For guests Thursdays 8 am-10 pm.
Riflemen's guild, Paul-Finkler-
Strasse, Tel: 32 77

Swimming
see Frankenfreizeit and indoor
swimming pool

Taxi:
Appler Tel: 20 00; Dänzer Tel: 44 05;
Ebert Tel: 72 27

Tennis:
From mid-April daily 8 am-12 am,
2 pm-5 pm, Tennis club,
Am Philosophenweg, Tel: 78 93

Theatre, cinema
Kapellenplatz – cinema,
Kapellenplatz 14, Tel: (09861) 46 58

Events
Information given by Tourist Office
Hiking: Marked round hiking paths
through the Tauber valley, over the
Engelsburghöhe (Merian panoramic
view of Tauber valley and hiking
map see p. 116 and consult Tourist
Office

www.rothenburg.de

Gesamtherstellung und © Copyright by
Schöning GmbH & Co. KG
An der Hülshorst 5 · 23568 LÜBECK
☎ (04 51) 310 310 0 · Fax (04 51) 31 03 130
E-Mail: info@schoening-verlag.de
Internet: www.schoening-verlag.de

Concept: Armin Rausch, Dielheim
Layout/typesetting: Yvonne Harth, Lobbach
Text: Wolfgang Kootz, revised and supplemented
by Karin Bierstedt

Photos:
Archiv Edm. von König Verlag & Mediadesign

Except for:
H. Kraft – p. 23, 24/25, 26, 27, 52, 54, 56, 57, 60 (below),
73, 74, 75, 91 (below), 96 (2x below), 97, 99, 100, 101,
102, 103
A. Cowin – p. 1, 4 (below), 12, 14 (below), 16 (centre),
17 (r.), 28 (above), 29, 35, 37, 42, 43 (above), 50, 51,
53, 55, 58 (l.), 64, 65, 66, 67 (3x), 69 (l.), 72, 76,
83, 85, 86/87, 88, 89, 92, 93, 94, 96 (above), 98, 111,
112 (below l.)
E. Schmitz – p. 16 (above), 71, 80/81, 107, 108
Imperial town museum – p. 40/41
Doll & Toy Museum – p. 58 (r.), 59
Medieval Crime Museum – p. 61-63
Rossmühle – p. 70

The following guides have already been published in the
same series: Nuremberg, Freiburg, Rhine, Heidelberg,
Black Forest, Dinkelsbühl, Baden-Baden, Munich, Berlin

ISBN: 3-89917-257-4
Ordner no.: 0162 0001